# CALLING

-VS-

# CAREER

*Embracing Your*
*Purpose*

DR. SANDRA HOLLOMAN WELLS

ISBN: 978-1-965082-26-3

Publishing By: DemiCo National, LLC

www.DemiCoNational.com

# TABLE OF CONTENTS

# PROLOGUE

Growing up in a small town inspired me to further my education. After graduating high school, I enrolled at Columbia Junior College and it is now referred to as South University. I was accepted and moved into Columbia Junior College apartments in August 1981. Classes started the third weekend in August, and I was off to a great start. Two weeks later, someone broke into our apartment and took all the money I left in the apartment. Since this was my first time living on my own, I was terrified and called my mother. She stated that I should just move back home and enroll in another school. My mom picked me up that weekend and I moved back home for the rest of 1981.

It was kind of depressing being back at home and I felt as if I had failed. While in high school, I stated that I would never attend Morris College. Never say never because God will make you eat that word. An application was submitted to Morris College and I was accepted. My journey started with Morris College in January 1982. It was decided prior to starting college that I would major in Business Administration. I was not exactly sure what career interested me and I was trying to figure it out. My first year at Morris College went well and I learned so much from my professors and peers. Also, I tried out for the basketball team and played two years. The interest in basketball was not as strong in college like it was in high school. My goal was to make my mother proud and finish college. I was going to be the first person in my immediate family to finish college and that was my motivation.

One of my college friends majored in education and she always talked about how difficult her classes were. It was not even a thought about majoring in education, because I wanted to work in corporate America and a business degree would allow me to do that. It was final that my major was going to be business with a minor in math. Some of the classes were very challenging, but I managed to complete the program curriculum. The most difficult classes were Accounting II and Business Finance. The professors for those classes did not have a life and they made my life very stressful. In May 1986, I graduated with a Bachelor of Science in Business Administration. Thank you, Lord!

# CHAPTER ONE

The job search journey began upon graduation from college. The first job landed was a part-time job working for a newspaper company. It was a chore going to work every day and I was not making enough money to put gas in my mother's car. I worked for the newspaper company for 6 months and I quit the job with faith that I would get another job. The second job was in sales selling World Book Encyclopedia and I never sold anything in my life. The sales position went well and it helped with my networking skills. This job lasted approximately one year, and I applied for a plethora of jobs. One day I was talking to my oldest sister about jobs and she stated that I should apply for a job at Lee County Department of Social Services.

I took her advice and researched job openings at the agency. I applied for a caseworker's position and was called in for an interview. The director, Mrs. Fannie Watson interviewed me, and we discussed my job in sales. One thing she shared with me that stayed relevant throughout my career was I quote "Always imagine yourself being on the other side of the desk", unquote. Even though it applied to that position at the time, it kept me grounded and humble in all my other positions. Several candidates applied for the position, but Mrs. Watson gave me an opportunity to work for the department. I was elated, because it was my first professional position, and my hire date was October 19, 1987.

My professional journey was a humble beginning and my salary was $14, 500.00 and I thought I was making a little money. Smile. Let us fast forward to 1989 and that is when Hurricane Hugo swept through Lee County. Prior to the hurricane, the state government was getting ready to reduce the workforce. I was going to be without employment due to the last hire first fired rule. It was the devastation of Hurricane Hugo that saved my job. I was so grateful to God for His grace that I was still employed.

The journey at the Department of Social Services (DSS) continued and it was going into my 3rd year at the agency. One day I went home with my colleague and her grandmother asked her a question about me. She asked if I was a teacher. My colleague said no, she works with me at the agency. There were times when I have met people and I would be asked if I was a teacher? Little did I know that those people were in tune with something that I was clueless about. The goal was to get the experience at DSS and move on to something bigger and better. God allowed me to stay there for 12 years. Several things happened during my twelve years there.

The first challenge was that my grandmother transitioned shortly after I started working for DSS. It was a difficult time for me because I was very close to my grandmother. I basically grew up in her house and we spent a lot of time together. Her passing created a huge void in my life because she was an amazing lady. She would always say "Take care of yourself and always be about your father's business". She really loved God and it showed by the way she lived her life. A few years later I moved to Florence, South Carolina to get away from the clients and get in a different setting. It was somewhat of a financial struggle driving back and forth every day and it became expensive. I was forced to look for a part-time job. The Lord gave me favor and I landed a job at a store called Casual Corner. The part-time job afforded me the opportunity to save money and have some supplemental income as well.

DSS was still my primary employment and my job title changed from Caseworker to FI Case Manager. The new title came with a pay increase, but we had much more responsibilities. It was always a challenge implementing new duties and learning new policies. There were stringent new requirements put in place for the clients that made it very difficult for Case Managers. I worked hard and learned those new policies and most of my clients experienced some level of success. It was mission impossible at first, but I managed to get all my tasks done timely and stay on top of my caseload. Working for DSS gave me a new perspective on life and how to be grateful for the little things. Sometimes, we tend to take the blessings that God has given us for granted.

The last major challenge during my time at DSS was when my mother transitioned. My mother battled breast cancer for about 3 years. She lost her fight with the horrific disease in September 1996. This was a valley place in my life and the grieving process was the most trying time in my life and Christian journey. I questioned God and wanted to know why He did not heal my mother. She was a Christian, a loving mother, hard worker, very giving, compassionate, she loved her family, and the list goes on. Maybe, her healing took place on the other side. The bible says in 2nd Corinthians 5:8 "We are confident, I say, and would prefer to be away from the body and at home with the Lord".

After my mother transitioned, I discovered that she knew I was going to marry the guy I was dating. My mother met Derrick in May 1996 and she did not say much about him. At the time, she was still recovering from her back surgery. She had a tumor on her spine and the doctor said the procedure may result in a 50/50 chance that the surgery would be successful. God is a healer, because the surgery was successful, and my mother was able to walk 6 months later. Praise break, Hallelujah! Unfortunately, my mother transitioned one year later. One of my mother's friends shared with me that they were talking about attending my wedding and Derrick had not proposed to me at that time. Derrick proposed approximately 9 months after my mother went home to be with the Lord. We were joined in holy matrimony on October 18, 1997 and we have been blessed with 27 years of marriage. According to Mark 10:9 (NKJV), "Therefore what God has joined together, let not man separate."

Two years after marriage, I decided to pursue a master's degree and become a career-changer. The decision was made to challenge myself in a different career field. The chosen field was Computer Resources and Information Management. After working for the Department of Social Services for 12 years, I actively started looking for employment that was in the city where I lived. As a professional, I absolutely hated speaking in front of an audience. It was easier for me to sing in front of a crowd, than to speak in front of a small group of people. In 1999, I was offered a job with Staff Development and Training at the state office for the Department of Social Services. The job involves public speaking, and this is the one thing that was forbidden. The position was challenging, and I was very uncomfortable training in the beginning. After the first two training sessions, the training position became my passion. The classroom gave me energy and I was an extrovert in those training sessions. Trainees shared several testimonials with me about how they enjoyed training and how they benefited from my experiences. Even to this day, I occasionally bump into former trainees and they share how successful they were as a case manager. Training gave me passion for the classroom, and I wanted to pursue a career in education.

In 2007, there was a supervisory position that became available in the training department and I was not considered for the position. The position was promised to someone who befriended the director, and she was not the most qualified person for the job. It was difficult working in that department with someone that had less experience. God allowed me to work with the new supervisor for 6 months. One day, the Holy Spirit spoke to me and said that I needed to start packing my office up. I walked by faith and not by sight, so I was obedient and started packing. In the meantime, I was actively looking for employment and no schools were calling.

Some days, I became a little discouraged and that did not cause me to lose hope. The middle miles were devastating to endure, and God was teaching me a lesson of patience. I wanted a teaching job like yesterday, but I had to wait on God's timing. He was preparing me mentally for the transition to the education field.

The summer of 2008 was on the horizon and I was crying out to God for a new career. One day, I was sitting in my office and I received a call from my husband. He stated that someone was trying to get in touch with me and he gave me his contact information. I reached out to the educator and he stated that I was the hardest person to catch up with. He shared that one of the schools in Richland One was looking for a Business teacher, because the previous teacher left abruptly. The educator instructed me to call the principal at the school about the job opening as soon as possible.

Let me reverse, the previous year I interviewed with the same school for a teaching position. They decided to select another candidate that was an alumnus of the school. I reached out to the principal of the school and he asked if I could come in for an interview on that day.

The principal and department chair facilitated the interview. After sitting in the interview for about 15 minutes, I was offered the Business Education teaching position. The principal asked that I let him know as soon as possible if I accepted the position. I told him that I would discuss the decision with my husband and get back with him. He stated, "Do you want me to talk to him?" and I said I will handle that. My husband and I discussed the position and I decided to accept the Business Education teaching position.

The next day I cleaned out my office and resigned from my Training Coordinator/Training position. The training position prepared me for the classroom, and I am grateful for the hands-on experience. The next week I attended the Program of Alternative Certification for Educators (PACE) seminar. I spent the next two weeks training for my new teaching position. The training was intense and information overload. The P.E. teachers were in our cohort and they were very entertaining. We had an amazing group of people and we had an awesome classroom dynamic and personality. Resources and experiences were shared every day. Several people in the cohort stated that I was the teacher's pet. The instructor would leave me in charge if he left the classroom briefly. It was fun to watch the "hate" coming from my classmates. I successfully passed the first part of the seminar. Instructors gave a pass or fail grade for each participant. We were given a journal assignment for the school year and it was due next summer. Participants were instructed to record daily activities in a journal. The business instructor stated that we should consider becoming National Board Certified. The seminar was a great prerequisite and preparation for the National Board process.

Two weeks prior to the first day of school, I had to organize and set-up my computer lab. The lab was in disarray and no one volunteered to assist me with getting the lab in order. My mentor did not introduce herself until after school started. I did as much as I could on my own and I asked for help. My brother-in-love, Carlton assisted me with setting up computers. He was treated to lunch for his help. All the business teachers worked in their classroom and did not concern themselves with the new teacher in the building. One of my home girls taught at the same school that year and we supported each other. If I discovered something new, I would share it with my home girl and she would keep me abreast as well.

It is August 2008 and the school year is getting ready to start. The PACE instructor recommended a book to read and the name of it was "The Ten Students You'll Meet in your Classroom". I read that book from the front to the back cover. The book enlightened me about the type of students I will encounter in the classroom. Even though I read the book, I was terrified on my first day of school. Teaching teenagers was totally different than training adults. During training we would take a bathroom break every hour, but that is not allowed in the classroom. Students would interrupt in the middle of my lecturing and ask to go to the restroom. That was baffling to me.

It took some time for me to adjust to the system, but after the first few weeks I was an expert. It was difficult dealing with the different personalities in the classroom. After the first few weeks, I realized some of the students had a story. They were not motivated to learn and did not want to be in school. The goal was to figure out how to establish a rapport with my students and hopefully learning would take place after students realized that I cared about their success.

# CHAPTER TWO

It was the first day of school and I was meeting my students for the very first time. We were on a block schedule with A/B days, meaning I saw my students every other day. Classes were 90 minutes long and lessons had to be over planned in order to keep students engaged during that length of time. The first day was spent introducing myself and allowing the students to do the same. Some of the students were respectful and some of them were trying to get a feel for my personality. I was responsible for teaching three classes and they were: Integrated Business Applications, Sports and Entertainment Marketing, and Keyboarding. Weekly, I was faced with the challenge of creating activities, assessments, and strategies for classes. Unfortunately, I did not receive any assistance or resources from my department.

I depended heavily on my friends who were educators in other school districts or if I had questions about the teaching career, I would contact them. Being a novice teacher forces you to learn new things. I was in survival mode after the first month of school, because I left a job that I knew and could do it effortlessly. My mentor was reactive as opposed to proactive. Information would be shared with me the day before the due date. I realized that I needed to be responsible for myself and stay abreast of changes and dates. This new outlook made my life less stressful and things started falling into place.

Thank you, Lord, I made it through the first quarter. The journey felt like a roller coaster ride, but I prayed my way to the first finish line. The next quarter was easier because I would multi-task and use my time twice. I did not eat lunch in the teacher's lounge, but I stayed in my classroom and graded papers or recorded grades. Grading during lunch cut down on the papers I would take home to grade. Papers would travel home with me and return the same way. I would be exhausted when I made it home.

The department chair stated that we should make the students work hard and not overwork ourselves. It took a while for me to figure that out, but I eventually mastered it. My lessons were planned from bell to bell and that eliminated discipline issues in the classroom. Too much idle time creates an atmosphere for distractions. Students were given bell work at the beginning of class before we would start the lesson for that day. The bell work is an excellent way to transition into the lesson. Students knew what my expectations were upon entering the classroom. The bell work activity eliminates some of the wasted time at the beginning of class and challenges students with critical thinking questions. The bell work would be open questions about the lesson that students had to elaborate on. The bell work was another way to introduce the standard for the lesson as well.

It is halfway through the school year and my confidence is building in the classroom. I was able to manage all my job duties and not take work home every day. Teacher's administrative duties can be overwhelming and very taxing. It would be a perfect world if teachers could just teach and not have to worry about administrative duties.

Fast forward. We are approaching the end of the school year and I am trying to finish strong. There are several things educators are responsible for when closing out the school year. Some things in my classroom needed to be packed away and grades finalized. I was given a checklist for end of the year requirements. Praise the Lord, I managed to get all my end of year procedures done.

There was another issue going on at the end of my first year of teaching. The state of South Carolina dealt with a budget crisis and some teachers did not sign contracts the next school year. I prayed actively during this time, because I was the last hired and would probably be the first fired. When I talked to God, I reminded Him that he placed me in the field of education. God answered my prayer and I signed a contract for the next school year. Hallelujah! Favor was shown on my behalf and I did not deserve it, but I thanked God every day. It was discovered later in my life that teaching was my gift. People would always ask if I was a teacher and I would say "no". Little did I know that I would be teaching and ministering to young people in the classroom. God is truly amazing and he always will prepare you for what is to come.

It is the start of school year # 2 and my comfort level is much better this time around. My classroom was organized, and I did not have to worry about that. I moved to the classroom next door because that teacher did not return. Fortunately, I received an amazing group of students the second year, but one student that joined my class a week later was a little difficult. He was in the teacher's classroom next door the previous year. That student was always hyper and very disruptive in the classroom. He always greeted me when he walked in her class. The student was in another business teacher's class at the beginning of the school year and she stated that he needed to find another class. It was by a divine assignment that he ended up in my computer class. When I realized that he was added to my roster, I was a little surprised. The Lord pricked my heart and I could not take the same stance as the other teacher who wanted him out of her class. I will change the name of the student and refer to him as Josh. He showed up for my class and God gave me the wisdom on what I should say to this student. I greeted him and he shared personal information about himself that I needed to know. We discussed how we would address those concerns during the school year. I shared with Josh my expectations and he agreed to those terms. Days he appeared to be very hyper, he would wait outside the classroom for 3 minutes and we would talk before he entered the classroom.

This simple strategy worked for this student and he was a nice addition to the class. I was challenged with teaching a new course and that was Animated Computer Production. The students created animation and used Adobe CS4. The course was fun and engaging for the students.

During the second year I was attending Columbia College and completed my 2nd masters. The graduate program was Divergent Learning and I earned a graduate degree in Education. The Divergent Learning graduate program was very user friendly for a new teacher and strategies that could be implemented immediately into the classroom. The program was designed for one year and it was very fast paced, but I managed to find balance and get the work done. Thank you, Lord! It was very taxing attending classes during the week, on weekends, and getting all assignments completed timely. By God's grace, I managed my time well and accomplished my educational goal. The PACE Program required that participants take 3 courses in education and I chose to complete another graduate program. It gave me a masters plus 30 hours and I advanced to another pay grade.

The PACE and graduate programs consumed my life from 2008 through 2010. While in the Divergent Learning program, one of my courses required that learners conduct a study on a student. We were asked to create a questionnaire with 20 questions and shared the document with the student to complete it. The student I chose was none other than Mr. Josh. I asked him if he would participate in the study if I kept his name confidential. Learners had to change the name of the student in order to maintain confidentiality. He was honored that I asked him to participate in my study and was enthused about the process. Josh was being raised by his grandparents.

The students in the computer class completed a journal entry daily and the topic one day was, please share your weekend plans. Josh stated to the class that he was going to visit his mother and I asked where she was. He stated that his mother was in prison. My heart dropped for him after I heard his response. The class was very respectful, and they listened and did not judge him or his mother. Kids can be cruel, but that was not the case with these kids. My response was, it is a good thing that you get to visit with your mother while she was incarcerated. By this time, I had heard Josh's story and knew why it was a struggle for him academically and personally. He completed the questionnaire for the study, and I was amazed about what was shared. He was thorough with his answers and returned the questionnaire in a timely manner. It was a pleasure sharing Josh's story and I received an "A" for the project.

After making the connection with Josh, I had established a rapport with him, and it was a pleasure having him as a student in my computer class. During the school year, Josh and I talked outside the classroom approximately 3 times. I shared with the teacher that did not want him in her class that he is participating and engaged in my class. We were approaching the end of the school year and it was the last day of school and Josh walked up to me and handed me an envelope. I was taken aback and did not know what to expect. I opened the envelope and it was a thank you card. The thank you card stated, "Thank you for listening to me and not handling me like my other teachers".

Those were powerful words, because I did not realize that I listened to him and gave him an opportunity. Josh taught me a lesson of being judgmental. The previous teacher judged him and did not give him a chance, but God changed my perception of him, and I was able to see him in a different light. I received several cards over the years, but that card is the most profound and meaningful one.

Prior to getting this amazing thank you card, I was dealing with if my job would be salvaged for the next school year. The school district was still dealing with budgetary issues and more educators would lose their jobs. I prayed and talked to the Lord and if I did not sign a contract that it would be alright. Let fast forward to the day of signing contracts and each teacher was called down to the principal's office. I was hopeful until the very end that I may sign another contract because the principal stated that he would try his best to bring me back for another year. When I walked into his office, he asked me to have a seat.

He stated that he was not able to provide me with a contract and ask that I sign the pink slip. It is official that I did not have a teaching assignment for the next school year. On my way back to my classroom, it seems as if I was having an out of body experience. When I arrived at the classroom, the teacher next door asked if I signed a contract and I told her "no'. She became very emotional and I told her that I was going to be alright.

I did not want to dwell on the negative and I was strategizing how I was going to change my prayer. I worked up until the second to the last day and I asked the principal if I could take off the last day of school. It would have been too emotional for me and I needed to get in my meditation space.

It's the summer of 2011, and I did not share with my friends and some of my family members that I was officially unemployed. This was one of those times that I needed to communicate with God for myself. At the end of June 2011, I received my last check and I contemplated if I was going to pay tithes from that check. I was obedient and paid my tithes. This is where I trusted that God would take care of me.

My husband asked if we should go on vacation and I stated "yes". I shared with him that I have earned it and we will go on vacation whether I have a job or not. My husband and I went on vacation and we thoroughly enjoyed ourselves.

# CHAPTER THREE

The entire summer was spent looking for employment and completing applications. Several of my friends asked that I pray for them to get a new job and I never shared with them that I did not have a job. I completed a virtual course at the State Department of Education for a potential online instructor position. Due to budget issues that job did not come to fruition. I am starting back at square one looking for another position. No one called me for an interview during the months of June and July. By this time, it is the second week in August, and I called my praying Aunt Marie and she asked me if I heard from any of those jobs I applied for. I shared with her that I had not heard anything. She stated that I should have heard something by now.

She encouraged me by saying that even though I had not received a call, God has a job for me. A week later, I was sitting in my family room and the Holy Spirit said look on the school district's website that I resided in. I said in my mind, there is no need to look on the website. The Holy Spirit tugged at me again and said look on the school district's website. The second time I was obedient, and I looked on the website and I saw a part-time job that I was interested in. There was a part-time After School Director position that was paying $35.00 an hour. I proceeded and completed the online application. Two days later I received a call for an interview from the Lead Teacher at the Magnet School. The interview was scheduled two days later, and I started preparing for the big day. I arrived at the school for the interview approximately 15 minutes before the scheduled time. The interviewer called me back timely and the interview went extremely well. At the end of the interview I asked when a decision was going to be made about the position and the interviewer stated, "very soon". There was a discrepancy when I did my SLED check, because someone in the state of South Carolina had the same name, but she was a different race. I needed to prove that I was not that person and that was a no brainer. Two days later I was offered the position and I was very excited to be employed again. It was the end of August and I started the job on the 29th. My work hours were from 3:00 p.m. to 6:30 p.m.

My duties were following the afterschool curriculum, supervised tutors & teachers, managed budget, etc. I was excited about learning my new job and meeting the students. They were an interesting group of students, because they did not know if they wanted to be a child one day or grown the next day. Most of the students had an amazing story and it was my assignment to establish a relationship with those students. The students were studying me and vice versa. Every day after school, I made sure students were in their tutoring sessions, so they may get the academic assistance needed. There were several components of the afterschool curriculum and I problem solved how we were going to accomplish all of them.

I invited several guest speakers, chefs from the district, entrepreneurs with a card business, and the students started a Step Team. One of the law firms in the city sponsored the Step Team and they were able to get uniforms. They practice every day for weeks, preparing for their debut. They performed at the afterschool end of the year program and at one of the high schools in the district as well. The Step Team gave those kids a sense of purpose and they looked forward to the practices.

The students were introduced to the district's chef and he made tacos with the students for his first visit. They were able to eat what they made, and the students consumed those tacos. The second visit the chef challenged the students with desserts. The dessert had to be colorful and tall. They had cool whip, angel food cake, and fruit toppings. Some of the students were very creative and they really enjoyed the experience.

We invited a Military personnel and he spoke to the students. At the end of his presentation, he taught the boys how to tie a Windsor knot. Most of the boys successfully tied the Windsor knot and a few of them needed assistance. That was a life-changing experience for some of the young men, because they did not have a clue about how to tie a necktie.

The students participated in a craft after school activity and they made Mother's Day cards. The company that provided the supplies assisted the students with designs and wording for their cards. The students were very creative and made beautiful cards for their mother or guardian. Even the boys enjoyed the craft hands-on experience.

The Afterschool program was a safe haven for the 68 students that we taught that year. One of the students shared that some of the kids tried to make out during the afterschool hours before I became the director. She told me that I was too vigilant and strict for that to happen. I shared with the student that it will not happen on my watch. My ultimate job was to make the afterschool program engaging and academically supportive for every student. One evening, I had to take a student home because her father was at work and could not pick her up. We called her father and asked if it was alright if I took her home, because it was almost 7:00 p.m. and I was ready to go home. The Afterschool Director position was rewarding, but I did not always get off on time. My day started at 2:30 p.m. and should have ended at 6:00 p.m., but that was not always the case. After working for about two weeks, I discovered that to complete my PACE Certification that I needed to be teaching kids. I was hired as the Afterschool Director and I coordinated activities for students, but I was not responsible for teaching them. The information was verified with the State Department of Education that I needed to be teaching students to complete my three years in the PACE Program. I shared with my boss that I needed to be teaching students, because I wanted to complete my certification. She stated that I will remain in the position and we will figure something out for you. The next week arrived and someone from Human Resources visited our campus. The human resource personnel welcomed me to the district and gave me a gift. I thanked the human resource personnel and she walked out of the building. My boss walks out and asks that I come see her after I get the students settled for Afterschool tutoring.

The students are all in tutoring and I graced my boss with my presence. She stated that she had a proposal for me. I said in my mind that was a good word and I was a little at ease. My boss said that she created a part-time teaching position for me, contingent upon me continuing working as the Afterschool Director. I was asked to teach a computer course and the class would be taught in the conference room. There were no available classrooms and we had to make the necessary adjustment. I agreed to the terms of the two part-time positions and we hugged on my way out of her office. I referred to the Lead Teacher (boss) as my guardian angel.

My heart was full of joy and I could not believe what I had just experienced. I could barely wait to get home to tell my husband what happened. On my way home that day, I was still processing how God blessed me. I found myself thanking God in the car on the way home, because God became a WAYMAKER on that day. HALLELUJAH!!! God gave me a personal testimony and I was grateful for that. When I arrived home, my husband was at home. I shared with him what happened at work and he was overwhelmed. He says, "did your boss really create a teaching position for you"? I told him, Yes! We thanked God for his favor and grace. Hallelujah!

My boss and I strategized about the number of students that would be in my computer class, resources, and classroom location. Books were donated from the high school next door and students had the resources they needed to successfully complete the course. Students had the option of taking another elective course. I had an amazing group of students and we learned from each other that school year. The students kept a journal and they shared stories about themselves. It afforded me the opportunity to get to know the students that I taught.

Several requirements had to be completed during the third year of the PACE Certification. Resources for the Praxis II were shared with me from my colleagues, I successfully passed the test, and completed my PACE Certification in December 2011. Praise the Lord!!! The PACE Instructor recommended that the cohort take the Praxis during the second year of the process. PACE participants had to successfully pass the test by the end of the 3rd year. God favored me and I met all the deadlines for the PACE Certification.

The school year of 2010-11 was a humbling experience for me. Whatever God wanted me to learn during that time, I felt like it was retained. I worked from 8:00 a.m. to 6:00 p.m. on a normal day. When parents were late picking up their child, I worked until 6:30 p.m. Thirty more minutes does not seem like a lot of time, but it is when your workday is supposed to be over by 6:00 p.m. By the time I made it home, I was BEAT DOWN. I was grateful for my jobs and by no means was I complaining. My assignment was with that population of students in that season and they blessed my life.

My boss knew that I taught online and she stated that I should share my credentials with the district's Online Coordinator for the Virtual School. I sent a cover letter and resume to the Online Coordinator and she stated that there were no openings at the time. Three weeks later the coordinator emailed me and stated that she had a course that came available and she asked if I wanted to facilitate the online course. My answer was, yes! I started out with about 5 students, but it afforded me the opportunity to experience another avenue in education. My journey started with the district's Virtual School in January of 2011.

The school year was coming to an end and I successfully completed my 3rd year in the educational field. There were some challenges during that year, but they were minor. The major challenge of my job is being outside during the afterschool hours. Even though I am a southern girl, I absolutely hate being outside. I did what I had to do for the job. The job kept me very active and I walked around constantly observing tutoring and activities. By the end of the school year, I was totally exhausted and was looking forward to the summer break. Thank you, Jesus!!! I shared with my husband that I was not going to return to the magnet school next year. He could not believe what I was telling him, but he did not respond. My desire was to get a fulltime teaching position at a high school in the district where I lived.

# CHAPTER FOUR

It is the summer of 2011 and I am living my best life. In the month of June, I started actively looking for fulltime employment. One day, I emailed this teacher I met while teaching online and asked her if there were any openings at her school? She responded by saying "NO". She used all caps which meant she was yelling. Every week I would check the district website where I lived and finally a position was posted. The position was at the school where I always wanted to teach. I would ride by the school and ask God to bless me with a job at that school. I completed the online application for the teaching position. The teaching position was for a Business Math teacher working with an Alternative Career Program. Math is not my favorite subject, but I felt comfortable with business math.

After completing the application, I received a call from the human resource personnel asking if I wanted my application sent to the school. I told the human resource personnel, yes. The next day I received a call from the principal wanting to set up an interview for the teaching position. We agreed that the interview would be scheduled for 11:00 a.m. the next day. I was so excited when I got off the telephone. I called my husband and shared with him that I had an interview at the school that was 10 minutes from our home. Praise God!!! There were several things I needed to do before the interview. I proofed my resume, created a cover letter, and meditated on what I was going to share during the interview.

This is the day of the interview and when I woke up that morning, I was finalizing what I was going to wear. It was extremely hot outside because it was the month of July in South Carolina. I am old school and I think women should wear pantyhose to a job interview. I wore panty hose, and it was about 95 degrees outside. I endured the struggle of being hot for about 1 ½ hours. I arrived 15 minutes before the interview scheduled time of 11:00 a.m. Approximately five minutes before 11:00 a.m., I was instructed to go into the conference room. Three staff members were in the room; principal, assistant principal, and the coordinator for the program I was being considered for. Everyone introduced themselves and we started the interview. I was a little nervous, but I felt good about my responses and professionalism during the interview. My question asked during the interview, how many candidates were being interviewed for this position? The assistant principal stated that three candidates were being interviewed. At the end of the interview, I thanked everyone and left the conference room.

On my way home, I called one of my preacher buddies and I shared with him that I wanted the position I interviewed for. Before the interview, I prayed and asked God to let me be considered for the job the same day. The preacher and I talked on the phone for about 20 minutes and he stated that he was trying to talk until I received the call from the school offering me the job. We hung up the phone and approximately 20 – 30 minutes later, I received a call from the principal offering me the job. Praise break! Hallelujah! I called my preacher buddy and shared with him that I got the job. We praised God over the phone! We were both going to start a new assignment that school year.

At this point in my educational career, I knew that teaching was a calling and not a career. A career is something an individual would like to pursue, but a calling is operating in one's gift or purpose. When I asked one of the staff members during the summer if her school was during any hiring and her response was "NO". I laid prostrate on my face that summer and sat in a quiet place. Several people asked me for prayer while they were actively seeking a new job. I never shared my dilemma and I just prayed for them. It did cross my mind that I was praying for someone else and I needed a new job as well. It was confirmed that I was not going to return to the Afterschool Director and part-time teaching positions at the Magnet School. God opened a door for me to enter and I am grateful for the opportunity. God's unselfish favor was shown that summer and I did not deserve it, but I was ever so grateful.

Even though I was excited about my new assignment, I had to share with the boss from my previous job that I was leaving. I waited a little while before I gave her a call. It was time for me to share my good news with my previous boss. I called my boss to let her know that I was offered a new position and I accepted. She says, why didn't you tell them that you had a job? She laughed. She congratulated and thanked me for what I had done for the students at the Magnet School.

The rest of the summer was spent preparing for the new job assignment. I was going to be teaching business math in an Alternative

Program that focuses on careers. I was a little apprehensive about the new course, but ecstatic about the new assignment. One week before school started, I attended a new teacher's workshop that covered information about the school's procedures. Everyone was very nice and supportive at the school. It is always nice when you receive a warm welcome for a new job. I was assigned a buddy teacher to assist with any questions or concerns I may have had my first year. My buddy teacher reminded me about things that were due and checked on me weekly for academic support.

It is the first day of school and I am meeting my new students for the first time. The beauty of my new assignment was my schedule had two planning periods and that helped me get through my first year. The previous teacher facilitated his classes differently and the students had to adjust to my teaching style. The math course was a progression and some of those math skills should have been a prerequisite. The math skill would be demonstrated first, and students were responsible for completing the lesson. Some days, I would be exhausted teaching the same skills several times. If students did not understand that concept after the 3rd time, I would work with those students individually.

One of the assistant principals discovered that I was available in the mornings and I sat in on IEP meetings about 2 to 3 times a week. If the Special Education department could not find a teacher, I was that teacher. Those IEP meetings became a routine thing and I had to make sure my obligations were being met as a teacher. At the end of the school year, I told the assistant principal that I should have my certification in

Special Education due to all my assistance during the school year. Of course, he laughed and thanked me for all my help.

Every student in the Alternative Program I worked with had a very unique story. My job was not to pass judgment, but I needed to get to know the students. One student that stood out above the rest was a female student with the most negative attitude I had ever seen. I will refer to her as Lisa. Lisa joined the class after a month of school, and she was kind of quiet when she first came to the class. She started voicing her opinions and they were always rude and negative. My job was to correct it and not embarrass Lisa. One day she became very disrespectful and I asked her to step outside the classroom. She had a meltdown and threatened to call her mom. I invited her to call her mom and stated that I would love to speak with her. She was sent to her administrator's office, so she could deflate and calm down. When she returned to the classroom, she had to apologize for her disrespectful behavior. I studied her behavior and she knew I was not going to tolerate the disrespect. She missed a lot of days from school and that was very concerning. Lisa had a lot of potential, but did not put forth her best effort. As we progressed through the school year her attitude became better. The 'aha' moment was when the class attended a picnic and they were with other high schools in the district. Some of those students were disrespectful and used profanity. It took all I could do not to address those behaviors, but they were not my students. My students observed those behaviors and did not say anything while we were there. When we returned to the classroom, Lisa stated that she knew why I was firm with them, and I almost fell on the floor. She was embarrassed by the character and attitude of those students from the other schools. Sometimes as educators, we feel like the students do not get it, but they rise to the occasion when they need to. Lisa taught me something on that day that firmness is very effective with students. They may not like you at first, but eventually they adapt to the environment.

There was another male student that did not invest into his education at all. I will refer to him as Lewis. He played around the entire school year and did not complete his online course that was required for graduation. We were approaching the end of school with two weeks left. Lewis completed a few assignments for the online course. He had two weeks to complete the online course or he would not be graduating on time. I did not make it convenient for him, so I required him to come to my classroom every day for two class periods and complete the online course. Lewis was fuming, because he did not like me as his teacher and did not want to be in my classroom. That was Lewis' personal problem and it was my job to make sure he successfully completed the course. He showed up every day and completed the course in one week. At the end of the week, Lewis thanked me and shared how much he appreciated my support. It was not about him liking me, it was about him achieving his educational goals.

There was a student that made me enjoy my first year at the new school. I will refer to that young man as Marcus. He was mature for his age and should have been in a magnet program. Marcus had wisdom beyond his years. At first, he came across as quiet and reserved. As the semester went on, I was privy to this student's story. He was being raised by a single mom and he was very respectful to me. He shared with the class one day how he was very disruptive and would shut a classroom down. Marcus stated how he appreciated me as his teacher and my passion for the students. He stated that I assisted students when they had questions about the lesson and demonstrated math skills for the class. Marcus would always refer to me as being "real". This was his senior year and he successfully completed all his requirements for graduation. Marcus was nominated for the "Turn Around Student". He had shown a measurable amount of growth over the last few years and it was very befitting that he received that award. I was extremely proud of him.

My first year on my new educational assignment ended on a good note. I established a rapport with some amazing administrators, teachers, and students. My Instructional Coach was a woman of integrity. She would visit my classroom every two months and leave a positive note to encourage me. I felt more confident every time the Instructional Coach visited. She was very instrumental and assisted me with questions about National Board Certification. After completing the PACE Certification, I knew that I wanted to complete the National Board Certification. I was completing school year #4 and I was qualified to start the National Board Certification process.

My first task was to pray and decide if I was going to actively pursue the National Board Certification. A teacher in another district stated that she assisted teachers with the certification, and she asked, "if I was going to pursue it"? We were approaching December and the application for National Board Certification was due in December. The application fee was $500.00 and it was going to be a sacrifice, because it was close to Christmas. This certification was viewed as an investment and an opportunity to grow professionally. At the beginning of December my mind was made up and I was going to accept the journey of National Board Certification. I submitted my application and awaited my approval for the process. The South Carolina Center for Educator Recruitment, Retention, and Advancement (CERRA) offered grant funding for educators wanting to pursue National Board Certification. I applied for the grant and was approved. Thank you, Lord! The grant was enough to pay for all entries for the process. Thank you, Lord!

# CHAPTER FIVE

During the month of February, I received the packet for the National Board Certification. I spent the first week reading the manual and familiarized myself with the procedures. The certification for Career and Technology had six entries and it would equate to approximately 60 pages of writing. My work was cut out for me. Exhale. I was ready to take on the challenge and complete the process. After reading those procedures, I contacted the educator that agreed to assist me with the process. We had a lengthy conversation on the phone, and she gave me pointers about the process.

I completed the first entry and scheduled a time for the educator to meet with me. She was late for the first meeting and we spent about 30 minutes reviewing the first entry. I thought the response answered the question with clarity. She recommended that I make minor changes and shorten the response. The word count was met and the response did not have redundancy. After our meeting, I made those changes. I moved on to the next entry and I did not let the educator review the second entry. She was contacted if I needed to ask a question and sometimes, she did not answer the phone. It was almost time to submit my packet for National Board Certification and I am in panic mode.

I contacted the educator and she was working on a technology portfolio and could not assist me. I was devastated and discouraged. My Instructional Coach was National Board Certified, and she agreed to read for me. It was last minute for her, but she kept her word. I spent a few days proofing my work and made changes. I was grateful for my Instructional Coach and her willingness to help. My packet had to be postmarked the following Saturday and I met the deadline. Hallelujah! The packet was submitted in April and scores were available in November. It was an extremely long wait.

In the meantime, I am teaching my students and praying that I will experience success with the process. It was my prayer that I will be successful the first time around. While praying about the process, I focused on other assignments at the school. Also, I was one of the advisors for the Gospel Choir at the school. Auditions were scheduled in the month of September and we had approximately 20 students participate. There was a lot of raw talent and we decided to keep all participants. Facilitating the Gospel Choir was like working with adults in a church choir, because the students came with the same kind of drama.

Choir rehearsal was scheduled three Thursdays out of the month; immediately after school. The students attended rehearsal regularly at first and kind of started slacking after a while. The choir had an event in the month of October, and we were preparing for it. We did not have a musician and songs were going to be sung acapella.

Some of the choir members were disruptive in class and they were asked to come by my classroom before the event, so we could discuss the consequences for their behavior. One student decided not to come by my classroom, and she showed up for the event on the following Saturday.

She was instructed that she could not participate, because she failed to honor my request. She stated, "I should not have paid my choir dues". Her tone was very disrespectful. I shared with her that she can receive her money back if she did not wish to participate any longer. That was a tough decision, but rules are put in place to follow and to discipline the students. I am a singer and I thought this would have been a great extracurricular activity for me. Advising became cumbersome and I knew that it would not be an activity that I would facilitate the next school year. I was also approached about coaching girls' basketball and I did not want to do that my first year at a new school. Gospel Choir was the only after school activity I cosigned on.

November is fast approaching, and I was getting nervous about my National Board Certification scores. The great thing about the process is that I only would have to retake the part I did not score high enough on. National Board scores are posted right before Thanksgiving. I decided to travel to Washington, DC with my husband for a football game.

He officiated in a college conference and traveled from time to time. It is Saturday morning and I received an email stating that scores would be posted by the next day. I was very nervous and did not want to look at my score, because I had a dream that I had not successfully completed the process. Finally, I mustered up enough nerves to look at my score and I did not successfully complete the process. I was only a few points away and very disappointed. I read in the National Board material that most candidates do not complete the process the first time. After reminding myself about that verbiage, I was not too discouraged. My mind was made up that I was going to complete the process.

At the end of the 2011-12 school year, I did not attend any professional development workshop that summer. I was at home enjoying my summer break and life. One of my co-workers called me and shared with me that one of the business teachers received a promotion and there was an opening in the Career and Technology Education Department (CATE). I was encouraged to apply for the position because my certification was in Business Education. It was difficult making the decision to leave the Alternative Program and go back to my first love. It was a joy teaching business and computer classes. There were less students and I taught the same class all day. It was the best teaching assignment I ever had, but I was not being challenged as an educator. The Curriculum Administrator challenged me to focus on my professional goals and not make an emotional decision. After our conversation, I decided to accept the Business Education teaching position and I was teaching the courses the previous teacher taught. The new job assignment was scary and exciting at the same time.

It is the end of 2012 and I decided to submit my National Board Certification application for re-entry. By this time, I had enrolled into a PhD Program and I wanted to finish the National Board process I started. Someone shared with me that one of the teacher's organizations gives scholarship money. I inquired about it with the teacher's organization and discovered that I could apply for the scholarship.

The scholarship application was completed the same week and a few weeks later I was called about setting up an interview with the board members. I attended the interview on a Saturday, and it took approximately two hours. Four board members conducted the interview and I was asked to write an essay after the interview. Three questions were given and I had to select one of the topics. It took about 20 or 30 minutes for me to complete the essay. Later that afternoon, I received a call from the president of the board, and I was awarded the scholarship. The scholarship was made payable to me and it could have been used for educational purposes.

Let me rewind a little. Some years back, my Aunt Marie prophesized that God said that I was going to get my PhD. In my mind, I was wondering why she was saying that. One of my educational goals was to receive my National Board Certification and I did not even fathom pursuing a doctorate degree. Going back to school was the last thing on my mind. Several of my friends were working on a doctoral degree and I would listen to their stories. One day, a representative from student loans visited the school and gave information about funding that teachers could apply for. After the session, I started researching doctorate programs and trying to decide if I wanted to enroll into a program.

The 2012 year was coming to an end and I had decided on a PhD program at Capella University. Classes started January 2013 and I was very nervous about the PhD journey. It was a little challenging getting used to attending school again. My life changed and school consumed all my time and energy. Assignments were due on Mondays and one assignment I overlooked and did not submit it. My professor sent an email reminding me about the paper that I did not submit. I was mortified and I do not know how I did not complete the assignment. It was one of the bigger challenges in the beginning, because I had to write 10 pages in one night. It was mission impossible, but I successfully accomplished the task. Going forward, I would always read my assignment section of the syllabus 3 times and all my assignments were submitted timely. The first quarter in school went very well and I received "A's" in my courses. It built my confidence and I told myself that I can do this.

After the first quarter, I worked on completing my National Board Certification that I started last year. I reached out to one of my co-workers and asked her to recommend someone to assist me with reading my responses. She referred me to an Elementary School teacher that assisted teachers with reading the entries. I gave her a call and she agreed to help with the process. She told me what her expectations were and how she would assist in the process. It was discussed that I would work on my National Board during the three weeks break from school. It took a week to complete the entries, because I wanted to make sure that I was successful this time around. God made a way financially for me to pay for those entries I was going to re-submit. Hallelujah!

My students were very supportive and participatory with the National Board process as well. I asked, who would like to ask a question on the video and to my surprise several students volunteered. It took two days for us to finalize the video. The students did an amazing job and they were very professional. They made me proud. It was the second time around, and I scheduled a date and time that I could meet with the reader. My entries were sent to her prior to the meeting and we discussed any discrepancies in those entries. Her certification was Early Elementary Education and if she understood my responses, the responses would make sense to the person grading those entries. In the first meeting, we spent 2 hours reviewing entries and making suggestions. There were minor changes that needed to be made and oversights. The first video had to be done over, because all the requirements were not identified in the video. I had my work cut out for the next few days. The students and I knocked out the video that Monday and I made of those recommended changes. After all changes were made, I sent the National Board portfolio to the reader and she proofread my entries one last time.

The reader approved all entries and the next step was to figure out how I needed to submit my entries. This was going to be the first year the portfolio would be submitted electronically. I printed the manual for submission and read it several times. The software needed to be downloaded and I needed to compress my video, so I would be able to send it. One of the IT staff members at my school assisted me with the software download and I was able to figure out the rest. Once I figured out how to submit the first entry, the other entry was very easy. It took about an hour for me to get every document uploaded and submitted. The electronic submission was easier, but it was new and a little cumbersome. I was very grateful for clear and concise instructions in the manual.

Exhale. My National Board Certification portfolio was completed and submitted. Thank you, Lord! It is time that I get back on my school schedule and focus on my PhD program. The second quarter was getting ready to start and I had to schedule a colloquium session during the second quarter as well. The colloquium session was an academic requirement session for the PhD program. I was responsible for the two courses and the colloquium as well. There was a ton of work I had to complete prior to the face to face colloquium session, but I managed to get all the assignments completed. It was a major challenge working my two online courses and the colloquium session.

My husband traveled with me to Jacksonville, Florida for my first colloquium. The colloquium sessions were very engaging and instrumental when deciding research topics. I knew I wanted to focus on a technology research topic, but I was not sure about what it was going to be. Before leaving the colloquium that weekend, I had decided on a topic and it was subject to change. I met some wonderful people that weekend and we shared information about our PhD experience. One day, the dean for the School of Education introduced herself in our class. She listened to some of the research topics and told one learner that she could not keep her topic, because it would be a violation to use patients. The learner had a meltdown and became very discouraged.

The professor asked me to share my research topic and the dean did not challenge my topic. Thank you, Lord! The dean asked me a question and I intelligently answered the question. Yes! She left our class and the learners breathed a sigh of relief. Going back home on Sunday, I was excited about my PhD journey and was convinced that I wanted to complete the process. My strategy was to successfully complete one quarter at a time.

The year of 2013 was an extremely busy year and I managed to get everything done that I started. At the end of the school year, I was looking forward to my summer break. It was easier for me to complete my assignments and I did not have to focus on teaching. My summer courses were interesting, and I was a little closer to finishing my goal. Hallelujah! Upon the completion of every quarter, I reflected on my goals for the next quarter and that strategy motivated me. It was like keeping an educational journal about your accomplishments and concerns. I am grateful to God that I had more accomplishments than struggles at this point in my PhD journey.

# CHAPTER SIX

It is the end of summer break and I am returning for the 2013-14 school year. This was my second-year teaching in the business department, and I had a complex task ahead. I was given 4 preps and my school year was going to be overwhelming and most of my time would be spent planning. The four courses were Marketing, Sports and Entertainment Marketing, Entrepreneurship, and Integrated Business Applications. Help me, Lord! It was frustrating thinking about how I was going to juggle all those courses.

Those marketing courses were different, but they were also very similar and some of the same activities could be used for both courses. That school year started with a lot of frustration. At the beginning of the school year, I was also approached about being the advisor for the Young Investor Club. My initial response was "no". I shared with the student that I was extremely busy and could not accept any other responsibilities.

The student asked two other teachers about advising the club and they said "no" as well. That student came back to me again and asked if I would reconsider advising the club. The student was an amazing young lady and she was very passionate about starting this club. I broke down and decided to assist with the Young Investors Club. I will refer to the student as Betty. She opened a Roth IRA account at the age of 14 and when I heard that I was impressed. Betty was serious about her financial future and goals. The CEO and founder of the Young Investors Club attend the Induction Ceremony. He wanted to surprise the club members and I did not share with the students that he was going to grace us with his presence for the ceremony. The first year 8 members were inducted into the Young Investors Club and they were the most amazing "Elite 8" I had ever worked with. I thoroughly enjoyed my first year working with the club and I managed to get everything done and then some that school year.

It was back to my PhD journey, because I managed several things that year. The second colloquium was scheduled in the month of September and that time I had more assignments to complete prior to that weekend. I was traveling to Jacksonville, Florida and I met some wonderful people the second time. One of the learners I met, we agreed to stay in touch and encouraged each other along the way. We wanted to graduate at the same time, but that could have been possible if our mentors worked at the same pace. We shared our personal stories and struggles while going through the process. We motivated each other to finish the journey and keep pressing. My professor that weekend was amazing. He talked about his doctoral journey and gave the learners a lot to ponder. One thing he said that stood out was, "Do not share this PhD journey, because everyone will not be happy for you". Only a few people knew I was pursuing my PhD and that was the way I wanted.

Sometimes, people are not successful because they share their stories prematurely. My PhD journey was shared on a need to know basis. My professor also talked about the Comprehensive Exam and my blood pressure probably shot to the roof. The Comprehensive exam had to be completed at the end of the course work and before going into the dissertation course room. The weekend was very productive, and the professor shared meaningful information about the process. My second colloquium was more effective, because I understood the process better and knew what I wanted to research. I made minor changes to my research topic and looked up references. We were required to have a minimum of 80 references. It became challenging finding references about my topic, but I just needed to change the keyword. The professor gave strategies on keyword searches and effectively using the university library.

At the end of the week, I felt more confident, motivated, and innovative. I walked away empowered and ready to complete my PhD journey. During the first and second colloquium, both professors stated everyone in the classroom will not complete the process. I spoke life to my situation, and I stated that I will be a part of the percentage that completes the process.

My second educational goal was to complete my PhD journey in five years. I was very fortunate because the university gave me credit for my Divergent Learning graduate program and all my courses counted towards the program. Thank you, Lord! Forty credit hours were accepted and that was a huge financial savings for me. I would have been in school at least another 2 years. I did not know if the university was going to entertain the question about accepting those credit hours, but I am very happy I asked. When I decided to pursue my PhD, I asked God to bless me financially for this journey. I successfully completed my first year of the PhD program and I was elated. Hallelujah!

The school year 2013-14 was a productive and blessed year. I was super busy, but two of my professional goals were accomplished. Several educators stated that National Certification was an excessive amount of work and they do not wish to pursue it. That statement did not deter me from wanting to accept the challenge of National Board Certification.

The National Board Certification meant that I would receive a ten thousand dollar pay increase in my salary and a nice plaque for my door at school. Also, the certification would enhance my resume and make me more marketable as an educator. There is a ceremony for new and re-certified National Board teachers, and this is where the door plaque is given. Teacher's names are added to the list of other National Board-Certified teachers on the district's website. The pay increase was given in two parts and I was so humbled by my success. I was proud that I did not give up and finished one of my educational goals.

In 2013, my Instructional Coach nominated me for Palmetto State Teacher Association (PSTA) Star Teacher. I had never heard of the recognition and did not know what to expect. The application had to be completed, a one-page essay, and three letters of recommendation. I inquired about the Star Teacher Seminar with my Instructional Coach and I decided that I would complete the application.

After completing the application, I received my letter of acceptance a few weeks later. The seminar took place in Seabrook Island, South Carolina and was scheduled for 5-days. My task was to get approval from my principal to be away from my classroom for one week.

I approached my principal in the hallway and shared with him why I would like to attend the seminar. PSTA was responsible for paying for the substitute and mileage reimbursement as well. After sharing the information with the principal, he agreed to let me attend the seminar. Yes! I was looking forward to the break from my classroom.

The seminar was one month away, and I had ample time to prepare my lesson plans for those five days. It was a little scary not knowing exactly what to expect for the seminar.

PSTA shared information about the lodging and set-up. What stood out was the limited internet access and I needed it for my PhD program. My contingency plan was to use my cell phone's hot-spot so that I could check my emails. The rooms did not have televisions in them and I was wondering how that was going to work for me. I was going to get the experience of a lifetime.

It was one month later, and I was off to Seabrook Island, South Carolina. I arrived around the scheduled time and I parked my car. When I walked to the building, I saw a sign that said, "Please keep the door closed, so snakes will not get in".

I started to get back in my car and return home. What have I signed up for? I was a trooper and conquered my fears and decided to stay. My room was on the second floor and our names were on the door. There were ten teachers from all over the state of South Carolina that were approved to participate in the seminar. We had a session scheduled that afternoon and everyone introduced themselves. We had a diverse group of teachers and many years of experience in the room. The facilitators covered information about housekeeping and meal times. Breakfast was scheduled from 8:00 a.m. - 9:00 a.m., so I decided to join the group for breakfast around 8:30 a.m. As I was leaving the building, I saw a deer near the building, and I walked back to the building. I was petrified about the wildlife out in the open. I waited for someone to walk me to the cafeteria for breakfast. There was a gentleman that was walking by and he walked me to the cafeteria. He could not believe that I was afraid of the deer. I wanted to tell him not to judge me, but I was grateful for his assistance. Smile. The next morning, I walked with one of the teachers to the cafeteria that rest of the week. I caught on pretty quickly.

The week was very relaxing, and I met some amazing educators that week. We all shared educational and personal stories. The teachers encouraged each other and I sympathized with some of the stories as well. One part of the week was very challenging for me. We went on an excursion and most of the information was about slavery. It was about the history of the city, but it was mentally draining listening to all the negative history. Every day we reflected on our day, but that day, we were not asked to reflect. I was ready to write down my emotions because they were through the roof. Another teacher and I talked about the excursion and how it made her feel. This was probably one of the best seminars I have attended, but it is not something I would recommend for every teacher. At the end of the week, I recommended on my evaluation form that the excursion be eliminated from the seminar and the effect it had on the atmosphere.

The ride home from the seminar was refreshing and I could not wait to get back home to my own bed. I was restored professionally and ready to pour into my students when I return to school. Upon the completion of the seminar, I knew teaching was my purpose and God placed me in the profession for a reason. Every time I questioned my transition to education, God would always give me confirmation about my reasoning for being there. The bible says that "your gift will make room for you" and I am a believer of that. God has made room for my gift and opened doors that man could not close. Thank you, Lord!

# CHAPTER SEVEN

Upon my return to school, I was purpose driven and ready to work on my God given gift. I was also more motivated to complete my PhD Program and move to the next level in my spiritual calling. The Star Teacher Seminar afforded me the opportunity to reflect and meditate on my professional and spiritual goals. God was preparing me for the next phase in my life and I did not realize the pruning stage was taking place. 2013 was a fruitful year, because I challenged myself professionally and academically. This was the year I started the PhD Program and submitted my re-take entries for the National Board process. After the Star Teacher Seminar, I was anxiously awaiting my National Board score. It was difficult trying not to think about my results, so I kept busy with school and my graduate courses. Also, I traveled with my spouse to football games at Morgan State University and Howard University to break the monotony and for a change of scenery.

The month of November had approached and I was counting down to the score release date for National Board Certification. Over the summer, I decided that I would schedule my surgery in November, because it was the end of the year and there was a holiday in that month. I would be out of work 4 or 6 weeks after the surgery. The surgery was scheduled for November 5th and I was approved for the Family Medical Leave Act (FMLA) for the time I would be out of work. I was a little apprehensive about the surgery, but I prayed, and God handled the rest.

Even though I was having surgery, my courses were still in progress and assignments were due during that time as well. I was proactive and completed assignments prior to my surgery date. Not meeting deadlines would have been overwhelming after returning home from the hospital. Grateful to report that my surgery went well, and I was released from the hospital on day #3. Hallelujah! God is still in the HEALING BUSINESS! (Hands raised.)

Now, I am two weeks away from the date for my National Board score. It seemed like every night I would dream about my score. My anxiety level was through the roof, but I tried to remain calm. Fast forward, it was the weekend of November 23rd, 2013 and this was the day that would tell the story. My score could be retrieved by looking on the National Board website. First, I prayed and proceeded to look up my score. When I logged on the website, I was shaking and had a difficult time clicking on the score link. When I say God will give you the desires of your heart, you better believe it. It was official, I had successfully completed my National Board Certification in Early Adolescence Through Young Adulthood/Career and Technical Education. Thank you, Lord! Praise break!

The first person I called after learning of my score was my reader, because she was a contributor to my success. When I picked up the phone and called her that morning, the first thing she said was "It seems like you are smiling". I stated, Yes, I am, and I shared my good news with her. She congratulated me and I was elated. The second call was to my husband, because he was in Washington, DC getting ready to officiate a football game at Howard University. He could tell I had good news based on my tone over the phone. My husband congratulated me, and we talked about how we were going to celebrate my success. The only thing I can say right now, God is faithful. (Hands raised.)

It was time for a praise break because it felt refreshing knowing that I had accomplished one of my professional goals. God placed the reader in my path, and she was what I needed to finish the National Board process. My message to you is that maybe reading this book, always consult God first and listen for His permission to move forward.

It was back to the grind with working on the PhD Program. The quarter was overwhelming because I was enrolled in 3 courses. Those courses were: Funding of Educational Institutions, Advanced Curriculum, and Instruction: Program Evaluation, and PhD Colloquium Track 2. My life was consumed by this PhD program and working a fulltime job. That was my life as I knew it, but it became a daily routine for me. Every day, I checked my emails and course syllabus for assignments. Did not want to turn in assignments late or not get them completed. It was the end of the first year of my PhD journey and I was feeling more motivated and confident as a doctoral learner. The confidence was there because I had an "A" average after year one. Thank you, Lord! It was necessary that I praise God while going through the journey and not after reaching the finish line. I was getting a little closer to reaching my educational goal. Hands raised.

Any assignment that God has ordained, He will order your steps and you will finish the course. My PhD journey was a faith mission and I trusted God every step of the process. There were times I was extremely exhausted, and I did not know how I was going to make it to the next level. God placed people in my path that encouraged and held me accountable for the journey. When I wanted to doubt what God can do, I would quickly be reminded by those guardian angels around me. My line sister and friend would always encourage me about the process, and she would say, "You got this, and I am not worried about you". Those words encouraged and motivated me to press toward my professional goal. The PhD journey is personal and should be shared with your support group because everyone is not going to cheer you on.

The journey was lonely at times, but I stayed motivated and excited about the outcome. There were times I had a plethora of assignments and time was of the essence. God would give me the wisdom to organize and complete my assignments. Participating in a PhD program is about organization and perseverance. Your life would be in disarray if organization is not a part of it.

Year #2 in the doctoral program was challenging, but not unbearable. Fortunately, I had 1 year under my belt and I felt confident and understood the journey a little better. The first quarter my courses were: Collaboration for the Improvement of Curriculum and Instruction and Advanced Instruction and Assessment: Theory and Practice. Courses were very engaging and rigorous. The major chosen for my PhD Program was very interesting. It allowed me to reflect on how the advanced degree would enhance my calling.

The next quarter the courses were: Advanced Application of Research to the Improvement of Curriculum and Instruction, Curriculum and Instruction Internship 1, and PhD Colloquium Track 3. My cup is running over this quarter and my anxiety level is through the roof. It was confirmed that I was approved to complete my internship hours at my school. The Curriculum and Instruction Administrator worked with me holding me accountable for internship hours. The expectation was to complete 500 hours within a 6-month span. It seemed like mission impossible, but it became mission accomplished. The administrator and I met and talked about my duties as it related to the internship. Duties consisted of serving on the Leadership Team, creating a Common Core resource website for faculty, observing job interviews and evaluations, working with summer programs, and other related duties.

The Leadership Team required that I attend meetings monthly and made curriculum decisions with the Curriculum & Instruction Administrator. Information from the meeting was integrated with professional development and in the classroom. The Leadership Team coordinated a professional development session for the faculty and every member participated in the delivery. My responsibility was facilitating the ice breaker for the session and it went extremely well.

It is a chore working with teachers because they can be very talkative and non-participatory. To my surprise, teachers wanted to participate by sharing their drawings and responses. They thoroughly enjoyed the ice breaker.

The Common Core Resource website was recommended by the Curriculum and Instruction Administrator who was my site supervisor for the internship. The task was to create a website with Common Core resources for all content areas. The focus for the district that school year was Common Core and the Leadership Team attended professional developments that shared information and strategies about Common Core Lessons. The Leadership Team's tasks were to create and share Common Core strategies with faculty members. The creation of the website was taxing and required lots of research for resources. Each content area had a minimum of 8 links on the webpage. The website was an on-going process, so resources were added throughout the academic year and teachers received more than enough resources.

During the summer, I worked with the Credit Recovery Program for high school students. The program afforded students an opportunity to recover the credit that they missed because of failure or lack of effort. Students would come to the school during the summer and complete an online curriculum based on the number of hours needed to recover the credit for that course. Students could only receive a grade of "D" and there was a cost for Credit Recovery. I worked with the Credit Recovery Coordinator and keyed data in the computer and assisted where I was needed. The assignment gave insight about the life of an administrator and I decided that I did not want to be an administrator. My skill sets would be more effective in Higher Education or conducting extensive research.

Once I completed the requirement for my PhD Program, it would increase my salary and my salary would be comparable to what an administrator earns. Fortunately, I would not have to deal with parents daily and carrying around a two-way radio. I could not fathom the thought of those duties. Other duties were assigned, and I graciously completed them. At the end of the internship, I reflected on my journey and what I gleaned from the experience. After observing my site supervisor, I knew I did not want to be an administrator on the Secondary level.

The Internship was engaging and very meaningful because I completed duties that were relevant to my PhD Program. That summer, I learned all the intricacies of administration and the demanding aspect of the job. After the internship, I had a whole new appreciation for the position because it is never a dull moment. Some positions require that the individual have lots of patience and that may not be one of my best qualities. The internship was an amazing opportunity and learning experience at the same time. Some assignments were tedious and time consuming, I would not change anything about the internship process.

# CHAPTER EIGHT

Grateful to God for all the blessings and opportunities I encountered in 2013. When you are in your season, God is moving and you are receiving. Always remember who gets the glory and that is God Almighty. God is my GPS and I obediently followed his directions. We should be guided and directed by the holy spirit and not our personal agenda.

I am matriculating through the PhD Program and becoming more confident with my courses. In the summer of 2014, I completed Statistics for Educational Research 1 and Curriculum and Instruction Internship 2. The Internship hours had been coordinated with the site supervisor during the break. I could not start my project until the quarter started, but I was prepared and ready to go. Some of the same duties were assigned and new duties because school was not in session and no students were in the building. Preparation for a new school year started before the end of the current school year. It starts in the month of March and continues through the summer.

The major challenge was the Statistics for Educational Research 1 course because I laid prostrate on my face while taking the course. My computer did not have the capacity to run the SPSS Software that was needed for the course. My husband and I had to make an emergency computer purchase and we were on our quest for a laptop. We visited two stores and I found a laptop at the second store. We purchased insurance just in case we had an issue with the device. My husband stated that "get what you want, because the device has to take you through your program". I concurred with his statement.

The Statistics for Educational Research 1 course was very complex and rigorous. I found myself reading my textbooks all the time to comprehend what I needed to know for each assignment. It was stressful strategizing about how I needed an "A" in this class. I was grateful to God for those professors who put tutorials on You Tube because they were my saving grace. Hallelujah! It was sometimes challenging creating statistical reading and reading results. I participated and submitted all assignments timely. It was a tight race, but I finished the course with an "A". Praise Break! Both hands in the air!

The rigor is being piled on during my second year. The next phase of the PhD program is completing the Doctoral Comprehensive Exam. After completing the 2nd Colloquium, the learners were told that the comprehensive examination must be successfully completed before starting the dissertation course room. My anxiety level had elevated to the moon and the unknown is always uncomfortable. Once again, I prayed and meditated during the break trying to mentally prepare for my task in the next few weeks.

It is Fall 2014 and I am enrolled in the Doctoral Comprehensive Examination course. I will refer to my professor as Dr. A., so I am not sharing her birth name. This professor was caring and very passionate about her teaching career. She made learners feel calm and enthusiastic about the comprehensive exam. Dr. A. thoroughly explained the process and answered questions we had. In this course, learners had 28 days to complete the exam and submitted it timely for grading. The exam could not have been entered late, because it would not have been accepted. It was due by 11:59 p.m. on the due date. I submitted my exam timely; It was submitted by 9:00 p.m. after I carefully proofed the exam several times. Once the exam was submitted, Dr. A. verified that she received my comprehensive exam. After receiving the confirmation letter, I called on the name of the Lord and prayed for a passing grade. The exam consisted of 3 parts and I wanted success on all parts. If I was not successful on any of the parts, I had to rewrite that part.

This process is like the National Board Certification and it prepared me tremendously for the comprehensive exam. When I reflected on my life, God was pruning me for this task and the PhD Program.

On November 19, 2014, I received an email from Dr. A. with the results of the Doctoral Comprehensive Examination. I am nervous beyond what you can fathom or think of. When I looked in the subject box, I saw "Congratulations". I opened the email and Dr. A. congratulated me for successfully completing my Doctoral Comprehensive Examination. This was where I yelled, "Hallelujah"! I know God will give you wisdom and knowledge to do anything even when it seems impossible. Hands raised in the air. The email also stated that I will be moving on to the Dissertation course room and that was a major accomplishment. Most learners do not make it to that phase of the program, but I made it and I gave God all the glory.

In the winter of 2015, I started the Dissertation course room, and I was scared and ecstatic. The unknown is always scary and motivating at the same time. My motto is "If the learners before me completed the process, I can do it too". This saying would always inspire me to keep pressing and reach the finish line. I could see the finish line, and nothing was going to get in the way of my journey there.

My mentor was assigned at the end of the winter quarter after I completed the Doctoral Comprehensive Examination. The mentor was responsible for coaching me through the dissertation course room and tracking my progress. The first Dissertation course room covered refining and finalizing the Research Plan. Tracks 1, 2, and 3 were completed and my research plan should have been ready for approval, but my mentor felt I needed to make some changes. My research initially was a qualitative study and participants were going to be interviewed for data collection. Once my mentor reviewed the research, she recommended that it be changed to a quantitative study. I was told that a quantitative study requires an extensive amount of work and qualitative study was more user friendly. I will refer to my mentor as Dr. J. She stated that a quantitative study was more logical for my research. Dr. J was the expert, and I was convinced that this was the way to go.

Revisions were made to my research plan and submitted to Dr. J halfway through the dissertation course room during the 1st quarter. She put her seal of approval on the research plan and submitted it to the Dissertation Committee. The research plan was reviewed, and changes were recommended by the committee. The first 2 quarters were spent

65

revising my research plan and connecting with my mentor. Dr. J was always very brief on the phone and precise, but she would always follow-up with me weekly. I prayed that God would give me a mentor that would be firm, encouraging, and motivating. With Dr. J., God gave me exactly what I needed to navigate through this PhD journey.

Fast forward to the 3rd quarter and my Research Plan was approved on August 3, 2015. Praise the Lord! Working on the research plan was mentally exhausting. It was imperative that dates are shared because my memory was taking me retroactively in time. At this point in the PhD Program, I was making progress and every level I completed felt like a major accomplishment. My husband and I celebrated the approval of the Research Plan by going to dinner that weekend. It was very therapeutic to take a break and have dinner with my spouse. I was super busy, but I would always make time for my husband and friends if they called. We should keep the main things the main thing. Nothing is so important that we cannot sacrifice time to spend with the people we love. I lived by this motto as well. Always make time for the people you love regardless of your hectic and busy schedule. You can always add a little more to your schedule.

My next phase in the process was to get approval from the Institutional Review Board (IRB) for my research. There was a digital form that had to be completed and it took 2-3 days. The great thing about the digital form was that it automatically saved the information. Documents were requested for the research on the digital form and that was why this step was so lengthy. Upon completion of the form, it was submitted and reviewed by IRB. The form was returned 2 times for minor things and clarification about the research. Those things were corrected and returned to IRB for approval. After the 2nd submission, my research was approved, and I was able to start the next phase.

This was where I was challenged with a hurdle because I needed permission to collect data in the district where I was employed. The data collection involved collecting data from 2 schools, 2 teachers, and 168 students. There was also a digital form that had to be completed and submitted to the Data Coordinator at the district office. The form was lengthy and required detailed information about the research. The first time the research form was submitted to the district office it did not get approved. The results were very discouraging, because I worked extremely hard on my research and I did not understand what the issue was. The committee met and decided not to grant permission for data collection. Here are a few lines from the feedback from the committee. "The committee has decided not to grant permission for your proposed study. The proposed research uses an experimental design in which students receive differing treatments."

Based on my research design, students would not be participating in an experimental design. I responded to the email and requested a meeting with the Data Coordinator. He did not respond to my email and I tried giving him a call. He did not respond to my request and at this point I am livid. I went to my principal's office and told him that I was going to look for a new job. It was insane that I was not granted permission to collect my data in the district where I am employed. I shared with my principal how I had been trying to schedule a meeting with the coordinator and he would not respond to my email. My principal said, "calm down and send me the letter that was sent to you and I will give him a call". My principal stated that he knew the Data Coordinator and he would find out what I could do.

That afternoon, I shared the letter with my mentor, and she stated that it was my responsibility to get permission from my district to collect the data. I spent the rest of the quarter trying to figure out what I could do to get approval from the district. It took one year to complete the research plan and I did not want to spend another 12 months modifying the plan. Totally changing the research plan was not an option for me. This was where I had to meditate and pray for guidance.

The next week the principal let me know that he had discussed my research plan with the Data Coordinator and he would be sending an email about the proposed changes to the research plan. I thanked my principal for speaking to the Data Coordinator on my behalf. He stated, "I want to see you get the paper".

God placed him in my professional circle, and he served as my guardian angel in this process. Two weeks later, I received an email from the Data Coordinator with recommended modifications. Recommendations were not feasible, and I needed to explain verbally how the research was going to be conducted.

Based on recommendations, I revised the data research form and re-submitted it to the committee. This time it took several weeks before I received my answer. I am in the next quarter and had not heard anything from the committee, so I reached out to the Data Coordinator wanting to know the answer. He responded, stating that the committee meets once a month and they were scheduled to meet near the end of the month. Fast forward, it is the end of the month and I am waiting on the answer from the committee. The revised research did not get approved and I was perturbed. Even though I am stressed to the point of no return, I laid prostrate on my face. I prayed all day and night about this matter.

One day, I was sitting in my classroom and the Holy Spirit said, "call the Data Coordinator" and I did. I picked up the phone and placed the call. To my surprise, the Data Coordinator answered the phone. I said in my spirit, Praise the Lord! I introduced myself and I know I caught him off guard. I personally requested a meeting with him, so I could explain my research and clear up any misconceptions. He gave me a date and time. At this point, I am excited about the meeting. I have 5 days to strategize about what to share about the research and proposed changes.

The day of the meeting had approached and I did not know what I would change if anything about the research. I meditated and prayed, but I did not know what I needed to say. I was on my way to the district office and I still did not know what I needed to say. My prayer was that God would give me what I needed to say, and I had faith and believed that. Right before I made the left turn on the road to the district office, God gave me the revelation about what I needed to share with the Data Coordinator. When I walked in the office, I saw one of the former administrators from the school where I work and we were talking while I waited to be called back for the meeting. The Data Coordinator walked out and witnessed me talking to the administrator that works with him. That may have worked in my favor as well. The Data Coordinator walked me back to his office and we started the meeting. I shared detailed information about my research, and I articulated the revelation God gave on my way there. The Data Coordinator looked at me and stated that the recommended change could work. I thought about my grandmother because I felt like running. I was overjoyed and I had never trusted God the way I did that day. I know God will come to your rescue and he will not forsake you. God showed up for me in a huge way on that day. Hallelujah! Praise Break!!!

My mentor was the first person I called once I returned to my car. When I shared my good news, she congratulated me and was excited for me. My mentor and I had established a great rapport and it made my dissertation journey purpose driven. She held me accountable and instructed me not to take a break. I was going to withdraw from the dissertation course room while waiting on the data collection approval and that was not the right decision. I did not make a lot of progress that quarter, but I became a prayer warrior. My mentor was driven and very passionate about her assignment as a mentor. After the celebratory conversation, she instructed me to move on to the next phase of the process. I kept pressing towards my goal.

# CHAPTER NINE

The last 2 years were spent in the dissertation course room and I was getting closer to the finish line. As I look back over the journey, most of the time was spent getting approvals and some of those steps could have been combined. The PhD Program requires that 16 milestones be completed, and I celebrated every time I advanced to the next milestone. On June 1, 2017, it was a glorious day because my mentor approved chapters 1 & 2 of my dissertation. Two chapters down and 3 more chapters to go. Thank you, Lord! Hands raised.

The summer of 2017 was dedicated to writing my dissertation. It was a challenging summer because lightning struck our home and the central air unit. The lightning struck the back right side of the roof and disabled the central air unit. We spent weeks negotiating with the insurance company about repairing the central air unit. We were without air conditioning for 2 or 3 weeks and it was in the month of July. It was HOT! My wonderful husband purchased a portable air conditioning unit and put it in the bedroom. At least, we were comfortable at night while we were sleeping. This was a crisis, but I was confined to the bedroom and my time was spent working on my dissertation. If the air conditioning was functional, I would have been distracted by other projects that needed to be done in the house.

The summer was slowly coming to an end, and I was consumed by the dissertation. It is August 7, 2017 and I received an approval from my mentor for chapters 3, 4, & 5 of my dissertation. GLORY!!! This was a major milestone because I have completed all 5 chapters. It appeared impossible initially, but the research and data collection made the writing achievable. My husband and I went to dinner with another couple, because the wives were celebrating their successes. We made reservations at this upscale steakhouse and the food was amazing. I am certainly not a steak lover, but I can appreciate a steak occasionally.

The year of 2017 was an accomplished time for me because I was recognized as the Young Investors Club Advisor of the Year for 2017-2018. The CEO of the Young Investors Club gifted me with a plaque and an IPad. It was a distinguished recognition after serving as an advisor for 5 years. There was a student in my Entrepreneurship class, and she wanted to start the club, but she needed an advisor to initiate the process. It was very impressive how she did her research about the founder of the club and she was super excited. I referred to the student as Betty in an earlier chapter.

She served as the 1st President of the club, since it was her vision and interest. The "Elite 8" were the absolute best group of students I ever worked with. There were 7 ladies and 1 young man. It was a pleasure serving as the advisor of the Young Investors Club after the first year. The "Elite 8" gave the word professional a whole new meaning. I accepted the assignment and added one more meaningful thing to my plate. Sometimes, we think that we cannot add anything else to our agenda, but I am here to tell you that we can always make room for one more thing. Fortunately, I served as the advisor for the Young Investors Club for 8 years.

Let's rewind back to the process of my professional goals. I was grateful to God that I was in a great place with the PhD Program, because my mentor and I submitted my dissertation to the committee. The next few months were spent waiting, getting approvals from the dissertation committee, and school of education. During this time, I have completed all the coursework for the dissertation course room, and I am currently not enrolled in a course. Correspondences were sent via emails, conference calls, and telephone calls. Reflecting on the dissertation course room journey, I completed a Plan of Action after each quarter. It was a chore in the beginning and then it became a reality. After the first 3 dissertation courses, I started making progress and completing milestones. The Plan of Action was an accountability strategy and it worked for me. The plan challenged me to anticipate what I wanted to achieve in the next quarter.

The university would send reflection cards annually for learners to record his or her goals for the school year. I would always complete those cards and put them where I could review them. It was a good strategy to write your goals down, because they can serve as a motivational tool for achieving your goals. Two years into the Ph.D Program, I came across a reflection card that I completed at the beginning of the journey. The card stated, I will complete my PhD Program and work hard to accomplish my academic goal. Looking over the reflection card made me a little emotional about what God can and will do in your life if you let him direct your path.

The fall quarter of 2017 was spent revising my dissertation and waiting on more approvals from the committee. The revised dissertation was submitted on October 31, 2017 and this was where I prayed and waited. The Dissertation Committee approved my dissertation a few days later. The committee reviewed changes and made their decision. Hallelujah! I was so close to the finish line that I could leap over it.

The next milestone after the approval from the dissertation committee was to defend my research. My presentation was scheduled on November 4, 2017 at 5:00 p.m. I was nervous that day and wanted to get the defense over with. My committee consisted of all females and they were distinguished ladies. That day, I worked a half day, because I did not want to be tardy or stuck in traffic. When I got home, I meditated and prepared for my presentation. I reviewed the presentation and note cards several times. I spent a lot of time with my dissertation for years and it became a part of my being. Just grateful to God that I stayed the course and did not take a break during the PhD journey.

It is November 4. 2017 and I am ready to defend my dissertation. Of course, I was on the conference call 10 minutes before the scheduled time and waited on the committee members. Two of the committee members joined the meeting at the same time and my mentor had difficulty joining the call. We waited about 5 minutes for my mentor to join before I started the presentation. My mentor eventually joined the conference call after I started, and she listened to the defense. Initially, I was very nervous and enthusiastic. My emotions were all over the place because I prayed for this moment. I was home alone, so I would not have any distractions whatsoever. Upon the completion of my defense, I asked if there were any questions and one of the committee members made one correction about the results of the data. Correction was noted. The committee had to decide if I successfully defended my dissertation. It was official that I had successfully completed my defense. Thank you, LORD! Hands raised in the air.

The next milestone was getting the final manuscript approved and submitted for publication. I cannot articulate what that moment felt like because things were happening like the flash. Two weeks later, the manuscript was approved, and instructions were given for publication. Yes! Two copies of the manuscript were ordered for my husband and myself. It was proper etiquette to order a copy of the manuscript for your mentor, but Dr. J advised me not to order a copy for her. She had access to an electronic copy of the manuscript and stated that she could use that if she needed it for future reference.

Instructions were followed and the manuscript was submitted for publication. At that point, I was able to exhale, because my work was done, and I was planning for graduation. The university granted me permission to order my regalia and complete the application for graduation. I was experiencing excitement overload because I had completed my professional goal. What started out as mission impossible, became a reality. Hallelujah! My mentor stated that I cannot refer to myself as DR. until the Dean approved the final manuscript. That was the rule, and I was alright with waiting for the official completion date.

It was January 30, 2018 and I received an email from the Dean stating that the manuscript had been approved. The dissertation title: "MULTIMEDIA INSTRUCTIONAL TOOLS AND STUDENT LEARNING IN AN INTEGRATED BUSINESS APPLICATIONS COURSE".

If I never publish another book, I can honestly say that a lot of tenacity and perseverance went into completing my dissertation. As I reflect on the journey, God directed my steps and placed me in a spiritual bubble. The bubble kept me covered and isolated to get the mission accomplished. I gave God all the praise and glory for that major accomplishment in my life.

I was making plans for graduation which will take place in New Orleans, Louisiana. In the month of December, I ordered my regalia, so it will arrive before the month of March. Graduation was scheduled on March 3, 2018 and I was counting down. The regalia took approximately 4 to 6 weeks to be delivered and I allocated more than enough time for the order. It was a super exciting time, but I was grateful to God for this educational accomplishment in my life. I could not articulate how I felt while waiting for this moment in my life. It seemed surreal. God was truly amazing! Hands raised.

It was the month of January and my regalia was received. The cap fit perfectly, but the sleeves on the robe were too long. I took the robe to my seamstress and she adjusted the sleeves before graduation. The alterations were costly, because those sleeves were huge, and alterations would be tedious. I picked up the robe a few days later, and the sleeves were fitting much better. The last thing I needed to order was a long garment bag for the robe because it was extremely long.

My flight was scheduled in the month of January and I did not want to check my luggage with the regalia in it for the flight. I did not want the nightmare of my luggage getting lost and not arriving timely. I took the regalia on the airplane with me in a long garment bag. Getting everything in order so I would not leave anything I needed for the trip and the commencement ceremony. Spoke to my mentor and we reminisced about the journey. Dr. J. was a drill sergeant, but she showed compassion and support when she needed to. She was the best mentor a doctoral student could ask for. I salute you, Dr. J.

The month of February was quiet as I waited for instructions for graduation. The university gave 4 tickets for the graduation ceremony and I had to request more tickets if more were needed. Two couples from my church family wanted to attend the graduation and I wanted to make sure I had tickets for them. Of course, my spouse was going to attend, and I needed 4 tickets for my church members. The situation worked itself out, because one of the wives could not attend due to another obligation and I had enough tickets for everyone. Based on the timing of the graduation, my family members were not able to attend and they were going to watch the ceremony virtually. That was my 5th graduation, and I was totally alright with that. My family had attended every graduation ceremony and this journey was personal for me. I knew my mother's spirit was with me every step of the dissertation journey, because God supplied all my needs during the process. Thank you, Lord!

The month of March had arrived! Excitement overload! I was preparing for the flight to New Orleans, Louisiana for graduation. Lord, I thank you for your grace and mercy. Most of all, I thank you for this accomplishment in my life. God, you received all the honor, glory, and praise. Hallelujah!

My husband and I landed in New Orleans on Friday morning and we picked up the rental car at the airport. We decided to stay a few extra days so we could see the city of New Orleans and do something fun. Marti Gras had taken place before our arrival and we did not experience that entertainment. The first thing I did was pick up my graduation packet and cords. If a learner completed the PhD Program with all "A's", he or she was given cords for Distinguished Graduate and I am proud to say, I was that graduate. Glory!

It was graduation day, and I cannot verbalize the humility and overwhelming sense of joy I felt. Every accomplishment I achieved in my life was because of the support system my mother provided. She financially supported my undergraduate degree and gave the parental support needed as well. My mother did not finish high school, but I would have awarded her a PhD in budgeting. What she did financially with my two sisters, and I was absolutely astonishing. She could have been a Certified Public Accountant due to her proficient mathematical skills.

Graduation Day was a moment of reflection and I was so grateful that God blessed me with an amazing mother.

It was graduation day and my spouse dropped me off at the front door of the arena. The graduates were sent to a large room and we were lined up for the ceremony. The School of Education had graduation at 11:00 a.m. and other content areas had different times. The ceremony was well planned, and it flowed like a charm.

The regalia was heavy, and I did not put it on until we were instructed to do so. I was extremely hot and praying that I would not be too hot during the ceremony. The best feature of the regalia was the nice hat, and it had a classy look about it. Some learners order the incorrect regalia because their bars were the wrong color. The university provided regalia for learners that were not represented correctly. I ordered my regalia through the university to assure that I purchased the correct regalia. The cost of the regalia was expensive, but it was all worth it. The regalia was the reward for successfully completing the PhD Program, and I was super motivated about getting to the finish line.

All the learners were lined up and we were ready to start the commencement program. Right before we exited the large conference room, there was this gentleman, and he was very emotional. He apologized about his state, but I told him that he did not have to. He reflected on his journey and sacrifices he made getting to that juncture in his life. My emotions were all over the place, but it was still a joyful moment for me. When we walked out of the conference room, my shoulders went up and my back was squared. The confirmation of the PhD Program was really happening, and it seemed surreal. I was thanking God after every step made. The faculty members lined the hallway to the arena and applauded the graduates as we walked by. My mentor did not attend graduation, but she watched it virtually.

As we were entering the arena, my husband and church members took pictures of me. They were able to get close enough to take nice and clear photos. The arena's lighting was kind of dark, but light enough to get great pictures with proper lighting on the camera. People are yelling and cameras are flashing everywhere. Graduates were all seated and the commencement program was getting ready to start. The president gave directives for the commencement program and we fast forward to the hooding. There was something funny during ceremonies. The professor that hooded the doctoral graduates must have been nervous. He was standing on a step stool, so he would be taller than every graduate. One graduate was about 6 "6" tall and he needed the stepping stool for him.

The professor was putting the hoods on too swiftly and they were looking kind of tacky. One graduate was very short, and the professor placed the hood on her face and moved her cap down. I can only imagine how disappointed she was with her pictures of the hooding. There was a photographer taking pictures during the hooding and another one taking pictures after graduates exited the stage. I was determined to help the professor get the hooding right for me because I wanted nice pictures of that moment. To my surprise, the graduation pictures were very nice. Since my last name starts with "W", I was near the end of the line. The commencement ceremony was coming to an end and instructions were given for the graduates' location after exiting the arena. My husband located me in the crowd, and we took pictures before leaving the arena. I had a lengthy walk to the parking garage, but my shoes were comfortable, and I was up for the challenge.

The parking in New Orleans was terrible because I wanted to try out a new restaurant downtown and we could not find a park within a mile radius. We circled the blocks for about 20 minutes and could not find any parks. At that point, I was frustrated and was shaking because I needed to partake of some food. The rest of the day, I wore my caps so everyone would know what I was celebrating. I did not want to take the cap off because I knew my hair would have been crazy without it.

My wonderful husband thought of everything for my special weekend. One of the ladies that we sat next to at the basketball game suggested that a Pandora bracelet would be a wonderful gift for my graduation present. She talked about how many Pandora bracelets she had, and they all had different themes. My husband acted as if he was not interested in her suggestion, but to my surprise he presented me with a gift back at the hotel. It was a Pandora bracelet. He purchased several charms for the bracelet and stated that I could add to the collection. I absolutely loved my bracelet.

# CHAPTER TEN

My husband and I stayed in New Orleans until Tuesday, so we could do some things we wanted to do in New Orleans. Of course, I went on a shopping trip and found some good deals and different fashions. We traveled to an outlet mall near New Orleans and we found some amazing deals. I treated myself in 2017 to my graduation car and I purchased a luxury car. After 30 years of working, I felt I could walk onto the parking lot and select what I wanted. The present came approximately 6 months before my completion date. I was taking the faith journey by rewarding my success.

It was Tuesday morning, and there was a monsoon outside. As we were leaving for the airport, my hair got wet and my hair was looking a little crazy on my way back home. That rain taught me a valuable lesson about never leaving home without a hat. Ever since that trip, I always travel with at least one hat. Every woman should have a contingency plan for her hair.

My Wednesday was spent relaxing and unpacking from my trip. It was time for me to think about my celebration party with family and friends that supported me through the PhD journey. My celebration date was scheduled in the month of May and we were winding down the school year. I was still riding on cloud nine thinking about what I had accomplished in 2018. It was impossible for everyone to attend the graduation ceremony, but they were all invited to the graduation celebration. It was imperative that the person who was with me for the duration of the journey attend the graduation ceremony and that was my spouse. Invitations were sent to family because that was the right thing to do and they were also sent to friends that were a part of the process. My educational journey was shared on a need to know basis and a select few people knew about the process. It was so much better that way.

The guest list consisted of 70 people, but I anticipated approximately 50 people attending the celebration. I wanted the program to be meaningful and impactful to the attendees. One of my former students was asked to minister a liturgical dance for the celebration. I will refer to the student as Lisa. She was gifted with the ministry of dance. She was given a song one year prior to the event, so she could work on her liturgical dance. I gave her a call in January 2018 letting her know the celebration was going to take place in May. She put the date on her calendar and made plans to be there. Lisa had wisdom beyond her years and it was a joy teaching her. After she graduated, we stayed in touch because I told her that I had a job for her to do and she would receive more information later. Four people were asked to give remarks and several friends asked to make toasts.

The celebration day had arrived, and I was preparing for my big night. My decoration crew assisted with getting things set-up for the celebration. I was fortunate because my niece came in early that morning and that was more hands-on deck. The theme was Mardi Gras, since the graduation took place in New Orleans. We had an issue with not enough tablecloths, and I asked my husband to purchase two more. He dropped off tablecloths and walked out quickly. To my surprise, they were plastic, and my blood pressure was off the charts. If you want something done right, you should do it yourself. We had a contingency plan and that was what we went with.

My husband and I arrived at the event about 1 hour before the start time. I wanted to watch my family and friends entering the building. I was super excited and very grateful for my accomplishment. One of my nieces was supposed to be the Mistress of Ceremony, but she was not able to attend the celebration. I was disappointed, but the celebration must go on. My brother-in-law was gracious enough to accept the challenge of Master of Ceremony and it was business as usual. A script was shared with him, so he would have some talking points and the outline of the program. He was chosen because he has impeccable public speaking skills. Let me just say, he did an amazing job!

The celebration was everything I wanted it to be and then some. It was well attended, and we started on time. There was one song that motivated me throughout the dissertation process, and it was "Dear God" by Smokie Norful. Every time I became discouraged during the process, I would listen to that song for direction. The song would put me in an atmosphere of worship and meditation. God would always give the wisdom needed to reach the next level. At the celebration, Lisa ministered a liturgical dance to that song. She was awesome! Program participants were great and shared candid remarks about the occasion. Some of my students attended and assisted with serving. They sacrificed their Friday night to help celebrate my success.

The most impressive part of the celebration was my husband's remarks. They were so endearing and very thoughtful. He shared how proud he was and his love for me. He was humorous and very distinguished that night. He hates public speaking, but I could not recognize it that night. He is only going to speak in public if it is necessary and that night was.

2018 was a year of accomplishments, completion, and celebration. If you put the work in, God will help you achieve success. Things were happening so fast and I was riding the waves. In the month of June, I was the graduation speaker at my church, and I was asked to speak the week of the Graduation Ceremony. It is always nice to receive speaking engagement at least 2 or 3 weeks in advance. God gave me a message for the graduates and students. When you are in your season, remember to thank God in the process. It is because of His grace that you are able to experience any level of success.

Later in the year, one of the school district's staff members asked if I would open my classroom to new induction teachers. I thought about it for a while and I said yes. I will refer to the school district's staff member as Dr. Q. She sent a follow up email with instructions and things those teachers wanted to observe. The new teachers were looking for lesson ideas, bell work routines, engagement strategies, assessment suggestions, and classroom management strategies. They also needed pointers on classroom procedures, transitions and making their classrooms run more smoothly. New teachers were all trying to find their balance with all the new responsibilities that comes with teaching.

It was an honor to participate in the Master Teacher Observation for two years. The first two teachers were females, and they observed my Entrepreneurship classes. Those classes were my first three classes of the day and they were 1st, 2nd, and 4th periods. Teachers observed all three and asked questions during and after class. Once students started working on asynchronous activity, I talked to teachers during that time. Every day my students would be given a journal topic to write about. It helps students come to order and get started on the journal. They would have 2 – 3 minutes to record their responses and students would share with the class. It took approximately 10 – 15 minutes for everyone to share. After journal reflection, I would transition into the lesson for the day and instructions or examples would be shared at that time. Journaling helps to establish a rapport with students and prepare students for business plan presentations.

As I prepared for the visit, I did not take the time to look at the name of new induction teachers. It was the morning of the Master Teacher Observation and the receptionist let me know that one of the teachers had arrived. She shared the name, but the name did not register with me. When I walked downstairs to the Atrium where the teacher was waiting, to my surprise, I knew her. We were members of the same sorority and I had no idea she was teaching in the same school district. I will refer to her as Ms. A. She was excited to see me and the feeling was mutual. We embraced and I walked her to my classroom on the 2nd floor.

We talked about her transition from banking to teaching middle school kids. Ms. A stated that she did not know if she had what it takes to teach middle school age kids, but I assured her that she could do it. I shared information about my previous career and that I was a Career Changer as well. It was Ms. A's first year teaching and she was trying to successfully complete it. I told her that one of the best perks of teaching is having your summers off.

The other teacher arrived, and I will refer to her as Dr. C. She was from another high school in the district and she was going to be teaching Entrepreneurship as well. The three of us introduced ourselves and talked about what they wanted to glean from the observation to integrate in their classrooms. At the beginning of every class, I introduced the New Induction Teachers to my Entrepreneurship classes. To my surprise, my students were on their best behavior and they participated willingly. Teachers were impressed how they came to order within a few minutes and started on the journal reflection for the day. It is a great strategy to manage your classroom and bring students to order when they enter the room. Initially, some of the students struggled with writing creatively, but eventually they came aboard.

The observation went well, and we reflected during lunch briefly. New Induction Teachers shared how they would use some of those strategies they observed in my classroom. They requested resources for teaching the business plan and I emailed them. I assured them that if they needed any assistance to reach out via email or give me a call. Teachers had to prepare for the second visit at another school. I walked them downstairs and they shared how much they thoroughly enjoyed the visit.

New Induction teachers were required to visit a veteran teacher's classroom two times during the first year of teaching. Master Teachers received a request to open our classrooms the second semester for New Induction Teachers, again. That time I did not respond to the email and two weeks later I received an email from Dr. Q. She stated that I was a hit because Ms. A wanted to visit my classroom in February, and she hoped it was okay. Of course, my answer was yes. I was honored she requested to visit my classroom a second time as opposed to visiting a different teacher's classroom. I told Dr. Q that Ms. A can grace me with her presence a second time. My task was to find the perfect lesson for the observation.

Fast forward to the day of the visit and I am walking Ms. A to my classroom. We talked during the walk to the classroom and she was so happy. We reflected on our successes and challenges in the classroom. Ms. A stated that she did not think she was cut out for teaching and I assured her that if I can do it, you can do it as well. She observed two of my Entrepreneurship classes that morning and she stated how much she loved my storytelling. One skill a great teacher must have is excellent story telling abilities.

Students would be instantly engaged if the lesson was connected with a great story or metaphor. After the 2nd period class, Ms. A stated that she was getting ready to leave. I walked her outside the door, and we embraced. Her parting words to me were, "Are you sure you have not been called into the ministry?" I said to her, go ahead with that. She smiled as she walked away.

Twelve days later and it is the beginning of January and I received an email from Dr. Q. The subject box was titled, Terrible News. I was so nervous opening that email. Below you will find the email.

"Hey, my friend. I am sorry to write with bad news, but I just got word that Ms. A passed away in her sleep last night. I am deeply saddened to learn this. It is just such a shock.

I wanted to share that she truly loved being with you and spoke so highly of wanting to be like you as a teacher. You made a definite impact on her and I wanted you to know." Dr. Q.

The rest of that day I was devastated and could not believe what I just read. Little did I know that February 7, 2019 would have been the last time I talked to Ms. A. She had a beautiful spirit and a zeal for life. That day I lost a sorority sister and the beginning of a long-lasting relationship. I visualized her in my mind all that day and those last words she asked me. It was so sad that she did not finish her first year of teaching.

I had to attend the funeral for Ms. A, because I was still in disbelief at her transitioning. My line sister and I attended the funeral service and there were several sorority sisters there to support Ms. A's family.

The funeral home was very small and we were packed tightly. The eulogy one of her line sisters shared was humorous and displayed what a free spirit Ms. A was. Even though she did not get married nor had children, her life was extremely fulfilled. The funeral service provided closure for me because I was struggling with the reality. I was going to miss the laughter with Ms. A. I was very grateful for the time I shared with her and the wisdom we poured into each other.

# CHAPTER ELEVEN

In the previous chapters, I wanted to share my testimony and educational journey. Teaching was not my career goal, but it is my calling. Every time I would get frustrated or discouraged, God would always send confirmation about where I was supposed to be. Last year, I had a brutal meeting with a parent about her son and she came to the meeting throwing punches before getting both sides of the story. Students should take ownership of their education and put forth the effort. This student was not putting forth the effort and complained about things he did not understand or wanted to do. I walked away from that meeting asking myself, why?

The next day I received an email from a student thanking me for being an amazing role model and outstanding teacher. After reading the email, I reflected on my meeting from the previous day. Every time discouragement would come my way, God would always send confirmation about where I am supposed to be. Working in your calling will not always be easy, but it is worth it. God has given me the weapon and ability to stand when things are difficult.

In March 2019, I was invited to speak at a Women's Conference, and it was an honor to share my personal testimony. After receiving the invitation, I meditated on God's direction for what needed to be shared with the audience I was going to speak to. Several months prior to the invitation, I taught several bible study lessons from a book titled, "If you Want to Walk on the Water, You've Got to Get Out the Boat", by John

Ortberg. I highly recommend this book because it challenges your spiritual journey. Chapter titles were: Boat Potatoes, Discerning the Call, and Focusing on Jesus. I spent time referencing bible study lessons and asked God to speak to my heart about what I needed to share. After reviewing lessons, it was revealed what the title of the messages should be. The title of the message was, "Out of the Boat Experience". The book covered several areas of my testimony and perfect metaphors were used as well.

The message title was confirmed, and I could create the PowerPoint presentation. It is important that I provided visuals and great storytelling for this message and testimonial. The first question I asked in the message, what is your calling? It was a rhetorical question for all the women in the room. A calling is something you seek God's guidance and not something you set out to do. I can recall how people thought my profession was a teacher before I ever entered the field. Teaching was initiated when I started training case managers. That was where I developed a passion for being in the classroom and teaching. My decision was made to take it to the next level.

Another thing shared with the group of ladies was that they should listen to their lives. God sends confirmation through dreams, opportunities, and others. We are assigned to a particular segment of the population and we must seek instructions about who they are. God will always make room for our gifts. A rhetorical question asked of the women, are you spending time with God? It made the ladies ponder the time they are spending studying and meditating on God's word. A metaphor was used from a sermon I heard 3 years ago. The sermon topic:

Meditation, Isolation, Separation, & Restoration. This young and vibrant female minister preached that sermon, and it came at a time when I was struggling spiritually. I was in the stage of isolation because I separated myself from ministry and operating in my gifts. Church hurt is like a scalpel that can cut very deep. As a Christian, I had to make the decision how long I was going to be injured or if resilience was the option. The minister's sermon moved my spiritual walk from isolation to restoration. I was ready at that time to be restored and gleaned from the experience of what God wanted me to learn.

Wrapping up my message, I asked one final question. Have you activated your gift? It challenged the women to seriously reflect on where God has called each one of them to serve. Wherever God has called you to serve, He will open doors and create opportunities for witnessing to take place. The fact that I was speaking at that Women's Conference was a testament that God will make room for your gift. It was my prayer to share my testimony about God's goodness and faithfulness. I did not know how and when it was going to happen, but my faith assured me it would.

The women's conference afforded me the opportunity to reflect on my personal and professional journey. They were so closely related, and it was intriguing how God was taking me through a process early in life. As I reflect on my journey, I understand why some things were not revealed during those times.

God was preparing me for great things to come. When the time came for the transitional segments in my life, I was ready to walk into my purpose.

The question is "Is teaching a calling or career for you"? If you are an educator and reading this book, please ponder this rhetorical question. It is alright if it is a career because some teachers love the job and perks that come along with it. Every time I questioned if I was supposed to be in the classroom, God would always send confirmation. Below you will find one of the most thoughtful thank you letters I have ever received.

*Good evening, Dr. Wells!*

*I just wanted to formally write you an email to say hello and I pray all is well!*

*I also wanted to send this email today to personally thank you for being one of the best teachers I have ever had. You have shown me what it is like to be a great leader, a great person, and most of all living to the potential that God has put us here to be. My first year at the school was my sophomore year, I had just had my first major move after leaving everything I knew behind. It was a very scary time for me, I was in a place where no one knew my name and I was only one kid in the crowd. After a few days in your class, it was clear that as long as I stayed quiet and listened, I would be okay. But as the year unfolded it was apparent that you were one of my favorite teachers. The way you took time to teach your student life skills and what it means to be truly genuine has stuck with me ever since. Ever since I left your classroom, I have been striving to become a better person, not only for myself but my community, my family, and strangers I face every day. It was so nice getting to visit you the times I did, getting to hear about your new son brought me so much happiness. I am grateful he was able to get such a strong and heartfelt leader that you are.*

*Throughout my life I have never been very religious just based on the fact that I have never experienced the proper guiding or messaging. But, about halfway through my senior year I had a very big shift in perception. I do not understand where or how it happened, I just felt different. I started to look at life differently, I started to realize that God sent us here for a reason and we all have a sole purpose to be here. Yet, I had been told this my whole life, it still was not clear to me until recently. I find my best side in serving other people. I find it sometimes difficult to take care of some of my needs but when it comes to other people, I chose to give all of my energy for the betterment of the other person. I am working to improve myself every day, but I am very passionate about sharing my love to other people. Of course, I do not know my true purpose yet, although it fueled my sense of being and made me a much happier person. I am still very young and have many more sights to see and people to meet but I got it down in my heart that everything that happens and everyone I meet is helping me mold into the man God wanted me to be. Whenever I go back and look to see who has made a difference in my life, I thank God for putting me inside your classroom because I don't believe I would not be who I am today if it had never happened. So, I thank you for being an amazing teacher and I thank god for giving me a very proper role model to follow.*

*Thank you again Dr. Wells, along with several other students, we have all been blessed to get to know you. Your work on this earth has been nothing but love and compassion. I hope to write you many more emails in the future. I hope you and your family are healthy and happy!*

*Thank you for everything,*

*Alex*

As a Christian, I never know when I am going to be entertained by an angel. The student was like an angel in disguise. It was a pleasure teaching and establishing a rapport with that student. Some students are assigned to certain teachers and I felt this student was assigned to me. Alex had wisdom beyond his years and it made my job easy and enjoyable.

I experienced a mind blowing day in the classroom one morning. My students knew what the expectation was upon entering the classroom. The journal reflection afforded me the opportunity to establish a rapport with the students and learn their names within the first two weeks of school. It was a chore initially for some students and after a few weeks they started appreciating the journal activity. The topics are content related most of the time and some generic topics as well. Students were instructed to share with the class what they would like for them to know.

One morning the journal topic was, Dr. Wells, there is something I would like for you to know. One student shared that she was depressed and she had been feeling down for a while. She stated that she needed to seek help for her depression. I asked her if she ever considered keeping a journal when she was in a valley place? She said, no. I recommended that she should write her feelings down and seek help from a professional therapist. The students continued participating, sharing their journal reflection and when it was over something interesting happened. Another female student asked if she could talk to the student that stated that she was depressed. I will refer to that student as Tee. She was given permission to step outside and talk to that student.

Tee walked outside and I gave the other student permission to walk outside as well. I joined them outside the classroom just in case an administrator walked by the classroom. Tee shared with that student about her experience with depression. She stated how she prayed, cried out to God, and He delivered her from the depression. At that point, I was in awe about what I was witnessing. I felt like leaping, worshipping, and running. Hands raised! Hallelujah! During the witnessing, Tee referenced her grandmother and how she introduced her to God. She stated that the devil is a liar and he could not have control over her mind. Tee stated that the devil cannot win and he is a LIAR! God showed me the anointing on that student and there was a glow on her. She had the gift of witnessing because what she shared with that student changed the atmosphere at that moment. The student she was witnessing and I started smiling. The heaviness was being removed and the student was being set free. Just one encouraging word from the Lord can make a difference. While this young lady was witnessing, I was having a spiritual metamorphosis. After she finished witnessing to that student, they embraced. IT WAS VERY POWERFUL.

This experience had to resonate with me before I could articulate what I had just experienced. I was led to share it with one of my colleagues that was not actively involved in a ministry. During lunch with one of my colleagues, I shared with her what I observed during 4th period. She saw me outside of the classroom with them, but she had no idea what was happening. After sharing with her about the conversation, she stated that I was the perfect teacher to experience that. I was so humble to hear and receive that coming from her. We should be a representative for God at work, home, church, etc.

Tee was being raised by her grandmother and I felt compelled to pick up the phone and call her. Teachers normally call home when students are acting out of character, but I was calling with great news. I shared with the grandmother how God used Tee to witness to another student and I was right there in the midst. God used her to say what I wanted to say in the classroom, but it happened the way it was supposed to. Being a teacher is so much more than facilitating a lesson in the classroom. The rhetorical question is: Is teaching a career or calling for you?

I pray that this book has minister to you and the space you currently occupy in your profession. It does not matter what career you have chosen,

God has placed you there for a reason. If you do not know what your purpose is, pray and ask God to reveal your purpose to you. Listen to your life and hone in on your passion. While doing those things, your purpose will be revealed. Thank you so much for reading my story. Until my next story, be encouraged.

The End

www.ingramcontent.com/pod-product-compliance
Lightning Source LLC
Chambersburg PA
CBHW061705120626
46550CB00003B/1092